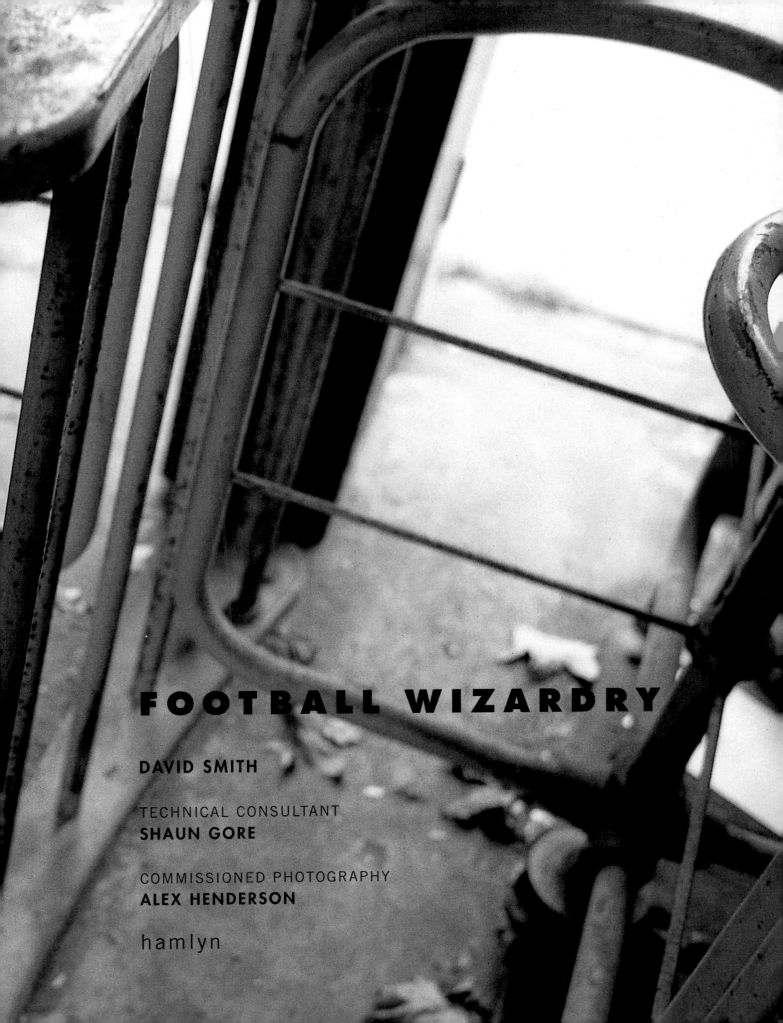

FOOTBALL WIZARDRY

DAVID SMITH

TECHNICAL CONSULTANT
SHAUN GORE

COMMISSIONED PHOTOGRAPHY
ALEX HENDERSON

hamlyn

Acknowledgements
Publishing Director: Laura Bamford
Creative Director: Keith Martin
Cover and Design: Vivek Bhatia
Design Manager: Bryan Dunn
Editor: Adam Ward
Commissioned Photography: Alex Henderson
Picture Research: Maria Gibbs
Production: Bonnie Ashby
Technical consultant: Shaun Gore

AUTHOR'S NOTE

There are many people to thank for their hardwork on this book. Firstly, I must thank Shaun Gore for his advice and assistance throughout the project. I am also grateful to Chris Pearce, Michael Cole, Laurance Batty and Paul Murphy for their good humour and patience during the three-day photo-shoot. I am also grateful to Tim Gardner and Umbro UK for supplying the kit for the shoot and the staff at the Varsity centre in Guildford for acco-modating us for three sunny September days.

EDITOR'S NOTE

Not for the first time, Hamlyn is indebted to Dave Smith for his hardwork and humour. In particular I am grateful to Dave for helping arrange both the photoshoot and foreword for the book. Dave also provided a true touch of footballing magic himself on the photoshoot when he performed a perfect Ardiles flick (on the run) wearing loafers.

SHINPADS

Many of the pictures in this book show players without shinpads. However, it is recommended that pads be worn in all practice and match situations.

LEFT AND RIGHT FOOT

All footballers should be comfortable using either foot. For this reason, a combination of left and right foot examples are used throughout this book.

First published in Great Britain in 1998 by Hamlyn
an imprint of Reed Consumer Books Ltd,
Michelin House, 81 Fulham Road, London SW3 6RB.

ISBN 0 600 59405 X

Printed and bound in China

BASIC TECHNIQUE 10

JUGGLING 20

PASSING 32

SET PLAYS 50

BEATING YOUR MAN 66

FINISHING 86

FOREWORD 6

WEAVE YOUR MAGIC 8

BASIC TECHNIQUE 10
Striking the ball correctly 12
First touch 14
Chest and thigh control 16
Heading 18

JUGGLING 20
Basic juggling 22
Thigh juggle and foot catch 24
Neck catch 26
Ardiles flick 28
Pincer flick 30

PASSING 32
Wall pass 34
Scissors pass 36
Power chest pass 38
Headed pass 40
Swerve pass 42
Disguised pass 44
Back-heel pass 46
Chipped pass 48

SET PLAYS 50
Long throw 52
Flick-up and volley free-kick 54
Bending free-kick 56
Passed free-kick 58
Whipped-in corner 60
Side-foot penalty 62
Chipped penalty 64

BEATING YOUR MAN 66
The dummy 68
Step-over 70
The drag back 72
The Cruyff turn 74
The Beardsley feint 76
The stop start 78
The nutmeg 80
Round the corner 82
Rolling foot over ball 84

FINISHING 86
Volleying 88
The Chip 90
Overhead kick 92
Scissors kick 94
Diving header 96
The scoop 98
Swerve shot 100
Glancing header 102
Power shooting 104
Sending the keeper down 106
Rounding the keeper 108

INDEX 110

During my seven-year England career I was fortunate enough to play in two World Cup tournaments. The skill on display was truly breathtaking and I have many great memories from both the Mexico and Italy World Cups.

Few things in football provide as much pleasure as scoring a goal, making an incisive pass or tricking past a bemused opponent. However, the greatest moments for both fans and players occur when a footballer produces something unexpected; a deft touch, a clever turn, a thoughtful pass or an innovative finish. These flashes of brilliance fix in the memory and remind us why we first fell in love with what Hunter Davies described as *The Glory Game*.

In my long career in football I have been fortunate enough to play alongside a number of prodigious talents who were able to produce the unexpected. At Newcastle, both Peter Beardsley and Kevin Keegan were among my team-mates. Both of these players were not only skilful but also industrious and I learned much from watching their lethal finishing and inventive passing at first hand. Following my transfer to Tottenham I shared the White Hart Lane midfield with two of England's most gifted playmakers, Glenn Hoddle and Paul Gascoigne. Though Glenn and Paul were very different players, both had incredible skill and the ability to turn a game. More recently, I've enjoyed playing with some of Europe's top stars, including Jean Pierre Papin and Eric Cantona at Marseilles and Marc Degryse and Dan Petrescu at Sheffield Wednesday.

Without exception, these talented individuals shared a genuine passion for football and have all worked hard to keep improving their game. I am also glad to say that they were happy to pass on their tricks and skills to team-mates.

Many of the crowd-pleasing skills demonstrated in this book have come about through the inventiveness of players like Gascoigne, Cantona and Papin. So whatever position you play and whatever level you play at, if you practise and perfect the techniques in this book you will become a more confident player and gain more pleasure from your football. No matter how well you close down, cover and tackle, without the Cruyff turn, the Matthews shimmy and the Beardsley shuffle, the game of football would be much the duller. I certainly wouldn't enjoy it as much.

Chris Waddle, Burnley, 1998

FOREWORD

"Football is not really about winning, or goals, or saves, or supporters… it's about glory. It's about doing things in style, doing them with a flourish; it's about going out to beat the other lot, not waiting for them to die of boredom."

Danny Blanchflower

WEAVE YOUR MAGIC

"I always felt that I was better than anyone else. It was up to them to get the ball off me, and they couldn't."

George Best, Manchester United, Fulham and Northern Ireland

The history of the world's best loved sport can be told through the careers of the footballing legends who have illuminated the game with their breathtaking skill. The modern view of Dutch football, for example, is as much shaped by Johan Cruyff's famous turn as by the trophies won by Ajax or the World Cup campaigns of 1974 and 1978. In just the same way, George Best and his extravagant skill have become synonymous with Manchester United.

The exploits of Cruyff, Best, Pele, Maradona, Platini and company have ensured that football remains the most popular sport in the world. The trickery of these modern masters has kept fans on the edge of their seats and opposition defenders on the seats of their pants for many years. Top players employ a vast array of attacking skills which grow ever larger by the season. Inevitably, these new techniques filter their way through the game to junior and amateur players, so now the Cruyff turn, the step-over and the drag back are used on parks, schoolyards, beaches and sports halls the world over.

Defensive techniques, such as block tackles and covering runs, are essential aspects of the modern game, but they do not have the same appeal as the trickery demonstrated in this book. All players, whatever their position and whatever their ability, would like to have the skill to control the football, bamboozle their marker and finish the move with a coolly taken goal. However, before you can turn a game with a spark of magic you must work hard on the training ground to develop your basic control, balance and technique. Without these three elements your attacking options will be limited, so get the foundations right and then you can start to develop your skills.

Football Wizardry demonstrates the key techniques used by the world's best players to bewitch their opponents and entertain their fans. With dedication and practice you too can perfect the tricks and flicks of the greats.

Franz Beckenbauer prepares to deliver
a pass with the outside of his boot.
The German sweeper was renowned for
his accurate passing which so often
launched an attack.

12 striking the ball correctly   **14** first touch

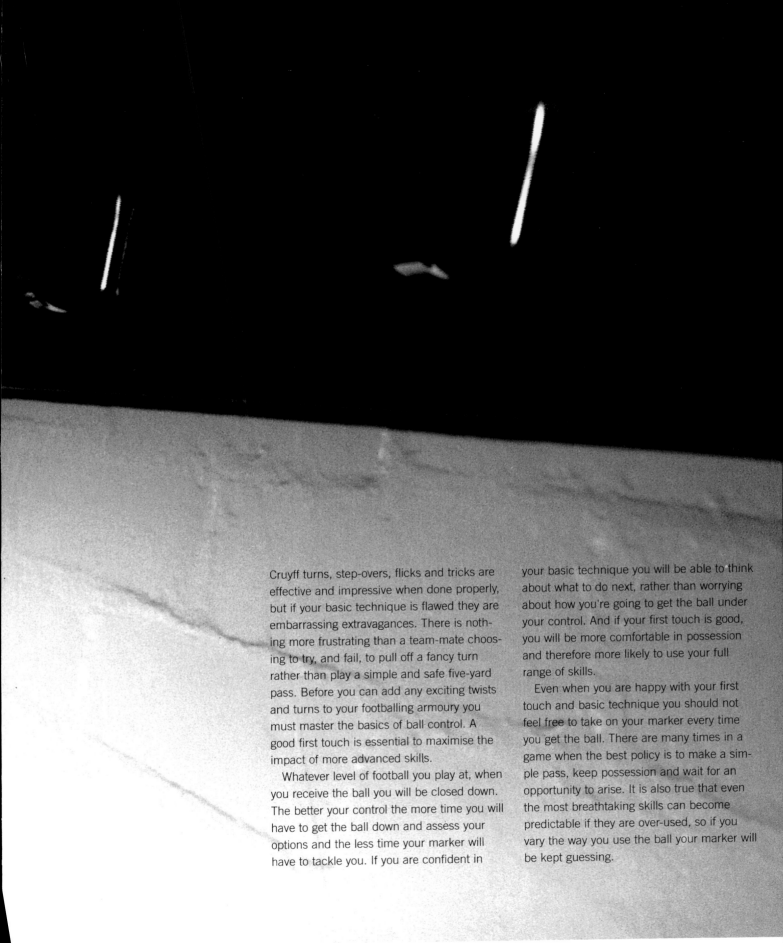

Cruyff turns, step-overs, flicks and tricks are effective and impressive when done properly, but if your basic technique is flawed they are embarrassing extravagances. There is nothing more frustrating than a team-mate choosing to try, and fail, to pull off a fancy turn rather than play a simple and safe five-yard pass. Before you can add any exciting twists and turns to your footballing armoury you must master the basics of ball control. A good first touch is essential to maximise the impact of more advanced skills.

Whatever level of football you play at, when you receive the ball you will be closed down. The better your control the more time you will have to get the ball down and assess your options and the less time your marker will have to tackle you. If you are confident in your basic technique you will be able to think about what to do next, rather than worrying about how you're going to get the ball under your control. And if your first touch is good, you will be more comfortable in possession and therefore more likely to use your full range of skills.

Even when you are happy with your first touch and basic technique you should not feel free to take on your marker every time you get the ball. There are many times in a game when the best policy is to make a simple pass, keep possession and wait for an opportunity to arise. It is also true that even the most breathtaking skills can become predictable if they are over-used, so if you vary the way you use the ball your marker will be kept guessing.

A   B   C

striking the ball correctly

The first art a footballer must master is that of striking the ball properly. Sounds simple, sounds obvious, but unless you get to grips with the basics you'll stand no chance with the more complicated skills which are outlined later in this book.

First touch and basic control are important too and these must also be made priorities. But, initially, the most important thing to concentrate on is being able to kick the ball correctly, accurately and with purpose. For the lucky minority, this seemingly simple act comes naturally from a very early age. For the rest it takes practice and, in many cases, a lot of persistence.

The technique of striking the ball effectively and keeping possession in a game situation is fundamental both to you as an individual and for the team you are playing in. To be able to pass to a team-mate with good weight and accuracy means feeling comfortable with the ball at your feet and being confident of making a good delivery. To have full control over the ball and make it go where you want to at the right speed you must do more than merely bring your foot into contact with the ball. Much more.

Wearing boots you feel comfortable in, using the right part of the boot to strike the ball, positioning your body correctly at the point of impact and knowing where you want the ball to end up; all these things are essential. If you don't master the basic skills you will never feel confident in possession and you will be in no position to attempt the skills outlined in the rest of this book.

i. Unless you have no alternative, avoid using the toe. This area of the foot gives very little control and accuracy, and nothing looks more amateurish than a hopeful 'toe punt'.

ii. Try to use the inside, outside, top or the instep of the foot in order to improve both the accuracy and power of your strike.

iii. Think about the position of your non-striking foot when attempting a pass or shot. It should always be next to the ball as it is struck; not behind or in front. Watch the top players in action and note their body position as they address the ball.

iv. Practise regularly – against a wall on your own is ideal – and remember to try and use both feet so that you are not totally dependant on one strong foot. Keep your eyes on the ball when striking.

Top tip

Even the best players in the world practise simple techniques on a regular basis. Eric Cantona could often be found working alone on the training field after his team-mates at Manchester United had left for the day.

A

The inside of the foot is perfect for accurate passes over short distances.

B

It is difficult to control passes with the outside of the foot, so practice is necessary.

C

The top of the foot is used to drive passes or make clearances.

1–3

The side-foot pass is the safest and most simple pass, but you must get your technique right. Position your non-striking foot beside the ball, strike through the ball (2) using the largest area of the side of the boot and control your follow-through to determine the weight of pass (3).

1

2

3

1

2

A   B   C

3

first touch

The ability to control the ball, using different parts of the body while under pressure from markers, is vital to all players. No matter how frenetic the game, all great players have time on the ball. This is because a true first touch gives you the opportunity to assess your options and make a telling contribution.

In most games, you will only have a matter of seconds to receive, control and pass the ball to a team-mate. If your first touch is poor, the ball will squirt away and you will waste time chasing it and you may squander possession.

Once possession is lost you have to work twice as hard to retrieve the situation. There are all sorts of ways, and numerous parts of the body, with which to control the ball. You should try to master them all so that you can deal with balls at any height and angle.

THE SIDE VOLLEY TRAP

A simple but effective method, and the most common because the inside of the foot is the biggest area of the boot you can use to control the ball. If carried out correctly, by watching the ball onto the large area of the foot and cushioning impact, the ball will come to rest close enough for you to make your next move.

THE TOP OF THE FOOT CUSHION

Using the top of the foot to control a ball dropping from a height is a difficult skill but when mastered is not only effective but impressive to watch. Position your foot early and watch the ball onto the top of your foot, and as the ball arrives try to pull it down.

ALTERNATIVE METHOD

The trap with the sole of the foot is one of the most effective methods. Keep your eyes on the ball and bring your foot down gently, yet positively, onto the ball. Do not stamp on the ball as this could result in it squirting from beneath your foot.

1–3
Get in position early and watch the ball onto the large area on the inside of the foot (2). Cushion the ball so that it drops into your stride (3) and move away with it under your control.

A–C
Controlling a dropping ball is a difficult skill. Adopt a good, early start position (A). As the top of your foot makes contact (B), pull the ball down toward you (C).

Milan star Paolo Maldini has an immaculate first touch which gives him time to use the ball effectively.

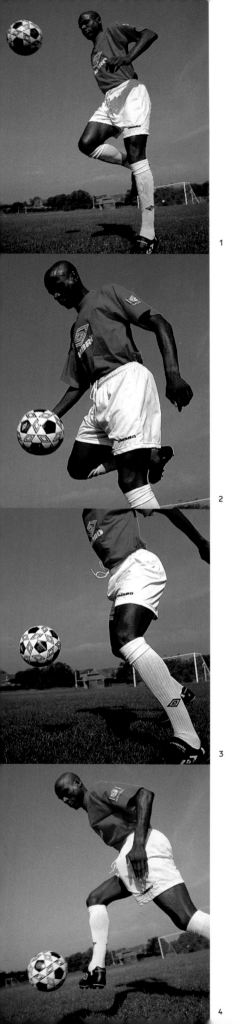

1

2

3

4

chest and thigh control

The technique for controlling the ball either on the chest or the thigh is much the same. It is all about watching the ball and cushioning it so that it drops nicely to your feet. When using the chest it is important to be in a good body position, on your toes and leaning back slightly as the ball makes contact with you. When the ball hits your chest it will begin to drop and you will be complete control.

When controlling the ball with the thigh remember to watch the ball until contact is made. Your thigh should be positioned at an angle of 45 degrees to the ground.

Tips
i. Keep your eyes firmly on the ball (not your opponent) as it approaches you, watching it onto your foot, chest or thigh.
ii. Whichever part of the body you use, always get into a good, balanced body position before you receive the ball.
iii. Make up your mind early and execute your move swiftly. Making the right decision and being confident of your ability to control a difficult ball gives you the edge.

Top tip
Find a wall and strike the ball at it, from different angles and at different speeds, to improve each method of control.

A–D
The chest can be used to control the ball in two main ways. For either option you should get in position early (A). To direct the ball toward a team-mate or away from a defender, stand upright and roll your shoulders to one side (B). Alternatively, you can lean back and cushion the ball into your stride (C and D).

1–4
When controlling the ball you will often be closed-down quickly, so use the large area of your thigh (2) to cushion the ball down into your stride (3 and 4).

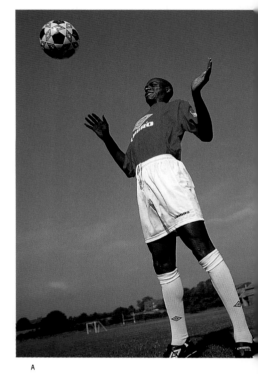

A

C

D

heading

Heading is one of the most neglected skills in football. It is also an extremely valuable skill. A player who is strong in the air is an asset to any team, but a player who can't head a ball, no matter how good they are on the ground, will never make it to the top. During a typical 11-a-side game the ball will be airborne for at least 20% of the time it's in play. If you can't compete when the ball's not on the deck, you're a passenger to your team. But don't despair – you can learn to head, it just requires practice and a little courage, at first!

The first hurdle to overcome is the fear of heading. Many players are unhappy about making aerial challenges – even some professionals will jump for a high ball with eyes shut, seemingly afraid of the impending contact, but don't be frightened of the ball! Head it correctly, using the forehead and with your eyes on the ball, and you won't feel a thing. Unless an opponent clatters you in the process, of course.

1–3
Watch the ball onto your forehead (1), bringing your neck forward (2) as you make contact (3).

1

2

3

The thing to remember is to be first to the ball and, most of all, be positive – you don't have to be a giant to be a good header of the ball. Colombian striker Faustino Asprilla stands at only 5' 9", but his powerful spring and ability to time his jumps make him a deadly adversary to even the tallest defender.

STICK YOUR NECK OUT AND PRACTISE

Heading is about confidence, timing and technique. And, as with any of the skills you will be shown in this book, it requires practice. Head tennis with a friend is the ideal way to develop your technique and confidence, always remembering that the point of contact, in most cases, is the forehead. This is the area you are going to gain most power from. The neck muscles will also help you in this respect. Watch any good pro going up for a header and you will see how he generates power and distance by bringing his neck, and upper body, into play. Tense your neck muscles as you bring your head back before attacking the ball with purpose. Don't just let the ball come onto your head. Meet it and follow through at the end for that extra yard, especially when clearing.

Tips

i. For most heading, the forehead should be used, as it provides both power and accuracy.
ii. Heading the ball should not hurt. So don't be afraid and always keep your eyes on the ball all the way to impact.
iii. Remember, it doesn't matter if you are short or tall, you can still head the ball. If you are shorter then you need to concentrate on timing your jump, judging the flight of the ball and getting a good spring at the right moment.
iv. Use the neck muscles and the upper body to gain power and distance. Your arms can help you gain height and will aid balance.

Top tip

A good way to improve your heading, and boost your confidence, is to practise jumping and heading a suspended ball. Also see how many times you can head a ball against a wall without it touching the floor.

A
Defensive headers are all about gaining height and distance. Get underneath the ball and head it upwards using your forehead.

B
The golden rule when heading for goal is to head down. Time your jump to get above the ball.

A

B

26 neck catch   **28** Ardiles flick   **30** pincer flick

1

2

3

4

5

22 basic juggling   **24** thigh juggle and foot catch

basic juggling

In the past many coaches frowned upon their players spending time juggling a ball around the training ground. 'You're not in the circus… that will get you nowhere in a match,' came the call from the touchline. Thankfully attitudes have now changed and the benefits of good juggling skills are widely appreciated.

The great thing about juggling is that it is a skill that you can practise on your own in a relatively small area. Developing your 'keepy-up' technique will improve your close control, balance and confidence when dealing with balls which arrive at an awkward height. It is also good fun.

Start by working on your basic foot juggling. Drop the ball onto your foot or roll it back onto your instep and flick it up, to begin the juggle. Once the ball is in the air, try to stay relaxed – don't plant all your weight on your standing foot, otherwise you won't be able to adjust your position to keep the juggle going. Strike the ball firmly (though not so hard that you lose control) with the top of your boot. Keep your eyes on the ball at all times. When you are happy juggling the ball on your strong foot try moving it onto your weaker foot.

Top tip
Watch professionals warming-up before a match. Many will juggle the ball to get their touch right.

1–2
Always keep your eyes on the ball when juggling. If you lose concentration the ball is likely to spin off the wrong part of your foot.

3–5
Control your strike to keep the ball at the height you want. It is also important to stay light on your feet so you can readjust if your touch is not true.

26 neck catch   **28** Ardiles flick   **30** pincer flick

1

2

thigh juggle and foot catch

FOOT CATCH

Keeping a ball up in the air is a difficult skill to master, but so too is the art of catching and holding a ball on your foot. The foot catch is a great test of control and balance. In theory, the skill is very simple: juggle the ball on your foot then, as the ball comes down, position your foot beneath it and pull the ball down cushioning it between the bottom of your shin and the top of your foot. Pull your foot up toward your shin to keep the ball in place. Sounds very simple, but the margin for error is slim – if you don't get your foot in exactly the right position the ball will slide off. The only way to perfect this skill is practice and lots of it.

THIGH JUGGLE

Juggling is all about innovation, so when you're happy keeping the ball up with your foot try using other parts of your body. The thigh is a perfect surface for juggling as it is wide and reasonably flat. Start your juggle with your feet and, when you have the ball under control, flick the ball up to chest height. Position your thigh at right angles to your body and strike the ball as it arrives at waist height. When you have mastered the skill with one leg, try switching the ball between each thigh.

1–3
The foot catch is a difficult skill to master. The art is to get your foot positioned beneath the ball as early as you can. Pull the ball down using the top of the foot and then catch it between shin and foot. Try to maintain your balance by keeping your standing leg flexed.

A–D
The thigh is an ideal surface for juggling. As the ball comes down, position your thigh at right angles to your body and strike the ball up. Don't just let the ball hit your thigh, otherwise it will lose pace and you won't have time to get your position right for your next touch.

3

A

B

C

D

26 neck catch

28 Ardiles flick

30 pincer flick

neck catch

If you are feeling really confident with your juggling skills, a great move to practise and perfect is the neck catch. Although this skill has no practical use in a match situation, it will teach you the importance of balance, control and keeping your eye on the ball.

There are two main ways to start this move – you can either, flick the ball up from a foot catch (see page 24) or juggle the ball on your forehead. Whichever method you choose the key is to get the ball moving over your head and to duck underneath it, watching it for as long as you can. As the ball arrives over your neck you must pull it down, lifting your head up to wedge it between your neck and shoulder blades.

INDIVIDUAL SKILLS

As your skills develop try to control the ball in as many different ways as you can. This will help you improvise during matches when the ball arrives awkwardly. The back of the heel is a good surface to control the ball as is the outside of the foot, but as with all ball skills control and accuracy only comes with practice.

1
Catch the ball on your foot and flick it up over your head.

2
As the ball moves over your head, drop your shoulders and cushion it into place.

3
Lift your head to catch the ball between neck and shoulder blades.

4
The ball is in place. Try to concentrate on keeping your balance.

A – B
As your confidence grows, try using other parts of the foot when juggling. The back of the heel is ideal. Concentrate on keeping your balance and be prepared to adjust your position if you mishit the ball.

26 neck catch   **28** Ardiles flick   **30** pincer flick

Ardiles flick

Flicking the ball into the air provides a golden opportunity to show your skills. Many professionals use a fancy flick to pick the ball up before taking a corner or a throw. These skills are really only for the training ground and, though of little use in a match, they are great fun and they look good. The most popular flick is associated with Osvaldo Ardiles who employed the overhead flick (shown above) to great acclaim in the football film *Escape to Victory*. The Argentinian midfielder amazingly used the skill in a match for Spurs some years later, but for most players this should be a 'training-ground-only' move.

1
Lean forward and drag the ball up the back of your standing leg (in this case the left) using the sole of the other foot (right).

2
As the ball reaches your calf take your right foot away.

3–4
Bring your left foot up, striking the ball up and over your head. Watch the ball over and onto your foot.

A
There are many variations of the Ardiles flick. This one takes the ball around the side of the player.

B
Lean away from the ball and roll it up the inside of your left calf.

C
Take your right foot in front of your body and bring your left heel up, striking the ball as it rises.

4

5

pincer flick

There are many types of flick up and all require different skills. To perfect the pincer flick you will need a good touch and fast feet. The ball is flicked up between both feet and, because it doesn't rise very high, you have to be very quick to get your foot back under the ball to control it. This skill will encourage you to react quickly and stand lightly on your feet. Pincer flicks are popular with full-backs who need to pick up the ball to take a throw-in, and it is also a neat way to start a juggle.

1
Position the ball between your feet, keeping your legs flexed.

2
Knock the ball with one foot onto the other.

3
Lift your foot to flick the ball into the air.

4–5
Adjust your position and get your foot back under the ball to start your juggle.

40 headed pass   **42** swerve pass   **44** disguised pass   **46** back-heel pass   **48** chipped pass

1

2

3

4

5

wall pass

There are many ways to beat an opponent who stands between you and goal. One of the most simple and effective methods is the wall pass (also called a 'one-two' or a 'give and go'). If carried out correctly this technique takes you past your opponent without the need for any dribbling or trickery. It relies, instead, on a team-mate reading your intentions and reacting quickly.

In five-a-side football a wall pass can be exactly that – a pass against the wall and around an opponent. The same principle applies in games played on open football pitches. The only difference is that you require a team-mate to act as 'the wall' to enable you to beat your man. This tactic is most effective when a midfield player passes the ball into a central striker on the edge of the box and continues his run to receive the ball beyond the striker.

Athletic, attacking midfielders, including Germany's Andy Möller and Italy's Dino Baggio, are the best exponents of this skill. These players run from deep positions and, unless their markers are willing to track all the way back and forward with them, they create chances.

Tips
i. Your 'wall', the person you are passing to, must know what you are planning to do. Develop an understanding on the training field and practise the move.
ii. For a good return pass from your colleague, you must give him a cleanly hit, accurate pass in the first place.
iii. Defenders won't stand back and admire your move, they will be after you. So you must be quick off the mark after playing the ball to catch them out.
iv. Make sure the ball is played wide enough to prevent the defender sticking out a leg to block the ball.

1
The player on the right has been closed down by the defender in white.

2-3
The attacker opts to pass the ball into the feet of his team-mate who, with his back to goal, holds off his marker and prepares to play a return pass.

4
The ball is played first time in behind the defender.

5
The first player runs onto the pass and shoots at goal.

40 headed pass   42 swerve pass   44 disguised pass   46 back-heel pass   48 chipped pass

scissors pass

This may sound a complicated move, but it is not, providing you follow some basic rules:

1
Face the direction of the pass with your back to the defender marking you.

2
Bend your knees and position your striking foot slightly behind your standing foot.

3
Just before the pass arrives make a small, one-footed jump off the standing foot, lifting the playing foot ready to flick the ball behind the standing foot.

4
Strike the ball with the largest area on the inside of the boot. Control the strike and never try to hit the ball too hard – you are likely to miss it completely.

At the end of the pass your legs should be slightly crossed, hence the name the scissors pass. Good timing, and speed, are critical to this move and deceiving your opponent. Try to disguise the move so that your opponent believes you are intending to control the ball and turn, rather than flick it to an opponent to run on to. When carried out on the edge of the opposition penalty area, this can often lead to a goal-scoring chance. It is also not as easy to predict as a wall pass.

above/right
Roberto Baggio gets in position to flick the ball around his left leg during a Serie A match for Bologna.

A–C
This skill is effective when used around the penalty area. Try to deceive your marker into thinking you are about to turn.

B

C

40 headed pass   42 swerve pass   44 disguised pass   46 back-heel pass   48 chipped pass

power chest pass

The chest pass is a skill usually associated with strikers and there has been no better exponent than Welshman Mark Hughes. He has not only the upper-body strength, but also the know-how and awareness, to bring a team-mate into play with an accurate, controlled pass under the severest physical pressure. In certain situations Hughes will leap to control a high ball on his chest rather than meet it with his head.

Brazilian Romario, too, has employed this particular art to great effect, preferring to move the ball on first time rather than slow the play down by first controlling the ball on the chest and then looking to pass to a team-mate, or turn towards goal himself.

This skill is ideal for a ball arriving at medium height which can be sent accurately toward the feet of a nearby colleague.

1
Keep your eyes firmly on the ball and also keep yourself between your opponent and the ball at all times. Hold your arms out to present a wider target.

2
Try and anticipate as early as possible the trajectory of the ball and position your body accordingly.

3
As the ball approaches bend the knees, lean back slightly and open up your chest ready to receive the pass, watching the ball all the time.

4
By thrusting your chest at the ball you can make sure your pass reaches a team-mate and is not intercepted by the player marking you. Note the position of the legs.

5
The ball falls nicely for an on-coming colleague who is suddenly presented with a goal-scoring opportunity.

34 wall pass   36 scissors pass   **38** power chest pass

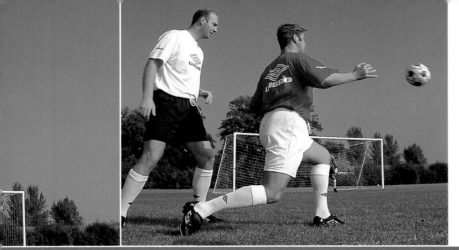

40 headed pass   42 swerve pass   44 disguised pass   46 back-heel pass   48 chipped pass

headed pass

Heading is not just for big, bruising centre-backs with the power to deliver 30-yard headed clearances, or for agile strikers who leap like salmon and score bullet headers. Heading can also be a subtle art for players of any size or stature.

Whatever position you play, at some time during the course of 90 minutes the ball will arrive at head-height. On most occasions your options will be simple – try to bring the ball under your control, or send a controlled, headed pass to a team-mate nearby. Trying to bring the ball under control with your head is a difficult skill and is made harder if you are under pressure from opponents, so in most situations your best option is to try to head a pass to a team-mate.

As with any form of heading, the forehead is the most logical part to use. The surface is bigger and flatter and gives you a good chance of controlling, or cushioning the ball so that it doesn't fly off at all angles. Of course, there will be times when you are looking to flick the ball to left or right, or behind you for a team-mate to run on to. In such cases the side or the top of the head are the best surfaces to use.

Few players employed the headed pass to better effect than Kevin Keegan and John Toshack when they were running riot for Liverpool in the 1970s.

Whether it was Keegan flicking the ball on for Toshack, or vice versa, the player heading the ball always seemed to be aware of the movement and position of his team-mate and the pair scored many goals as a result.

In the modern game, England's Teddy Sheringham is a very intelligent link-up player and uses his head in more ways than one to create openings for team-mates. Sheringham is particularly dangerous at set plays – free-kicks around the box and corners – and has great awareness of team-mates who are in better positions. If the angle is too tight for Sheringham to head for goal, he will invariably head the ball back toward the danger zone for a colleague to finish off the move. Defensively, German stopper Jürgen Kohler has been one of the best exponents of the headed pass in world football for many years.

34 wall pass   36 scissors pass   38 power chest pass

3

4

Tips

i. Always keep your eyes on the ball until you have delivered your pass.

ii. Make up your mind where you are going to head the ball, and to whom, and position your head and body ready to direct the pass.

iii. Balance is all-important, as is the ability to control the pace of the ball.

iv. Unlike defensive headers or goal attempts, the headed pass needs to be cushioned so the neck and shoulder muscles should be relaxed.

v. Allow the ball to come on to the forehead rather than meeting it with power. Remember, the direction of your header is essential.

1

The striker on the right of this picture has 'no angle' to head for goal.

2

He gets up early and directs his header back toward a team-mate.

3–4

The ball is sent down to the feet of the oncoming player who is able to strike for goal (4).

swerve pass

Christian Ziege in action for his country. The attacking left-back became a regular in the national team in the mid 1990s following outstanding displays for Bayern Munich.

Ziege, hard at work on his club's training ground, practises bending the ball around a plastic wall.

The side-foot pass is the safest and one of the most effective deliveries you can make, but it is not always an option. Sometimes it is impossible to find a team-mate with a direct pass along the ground. One solution may be the swerve pass. The art of bending or curling the ball around obstacles – a favoured skill of full-backs.

There are two types of swerved pass – one hit with the inside of the boot which, for a right-footed player will arc the ball from right to left, and the other with the outside of the boot which, again taking the example of a right-footer, will curl from left to right. The margin for error when hitting a pass with the inside of the foot is less than that which applies to striking a ball with the outside. Either way, both skills require much practice.

The swerve pass is commonly used to avoid an opponent standing in front of a full-back who is trying to pass to a winger standing further along the touch-line.

Along with forwards such as Gianfranco Zola and David Ginola, the modern breed of attacking defenders like Christian Ziege and Winston Bogarde are shining examples of the type of player who make good use of this particular skill. All of these players are blessed with immense natural talent, but this does not stop them from spending hours on the practice ground improving their skills. With enough practice you too could add the swerve pass to your game.

1

34 wall pass **36** scissors pass **38** power chest pass

1
Keep your eye on the ball as you run in.

2
Graze across the ball, aiming slightly wide of the intended target.

3
The player has brought his right leg across his body to impart the necessary spin.

2

3

Tips

i. When striking the ball with the inside of the foot, 'graze' the ball rather than strike right through it.

ii. The worst thing you can do is under-hit the pass and not even get the ball around your opponent. Strike the ball cleanly and with confidence.

iii. In order to get the maximum amount of bend on the ball, exaggerate your follow-through.

iv. Remember that passing is not just about finding a team-mate but presenting him with a ball he can control comfortably and then use effectively.

40 headed pass   **42 swerve pass**   44 disguised pass   46 back-heel pass   48 chipped pass

1

2

disguised pass

You may not be blessed with the agility and looseness of limb to carry out the most extreme of disguised passes – the reverse pass, but with practice anybody can perfect a simple disguised pass.

This skill is particularly useful when running with the ball, closely guarded by a vigilant opponent, and without a team-mate in easy passing range. You appear to be running further and further into trouble, and you're probably running out of space too. In most cases players will try to change direction, but your marker will be expecting this. The alternative is to cut the ball back in the opposite direction to that which you are running in and into the path of a team-mate.

To use this skill you will need good balance and the ability to change the direction of play by re-adjusting your body position and wrapping your foot around the ball in order to make the pass. The key to this technique, however, is an understanding of the runs your team-mates will make and an awareness of what is going on around you.

Smaller players with fleet of foot such as Peter Beardsley, Diego Maradona and Gianfranco Zola seem able to twist, turn and release reverse passes from dead-end runs which were going nowhere.

1

The player in red appears to be going nowhere as the opponent closes down his space, preventing him going wider or further upfield.

2

Hearing a shout from a team-mate, he prepares to take his only route out of trouble. However, he does not show any sign that he plans to cut the ball back.

3

He begins to adjust his body position, with his standing foot directly behind the ball. His eyes remain on the ball and not the opponent or his team-mate.

4

By wrapping his striking foot around the ball and bringing the leg around at a sharp angle he is now in a better position to whip the ball back to his team-mate.

5

With a sideways, jabbing movement the player brings his striking leg down sharply to direct a pass away from the defender with the inside of the foot.

6

The pass is perfect and suddenly the defender, having looked favourite to win the ball, is caught out.

left

Diego Maradona combined wonderful balance and trickery with superb passing skills. The Argentinian maestro was able to weave his way through opposing defences without breaking sweat.

40 headed pass   42 swerve pass   **44 disguised pass**   46 back-heel pass   48 chipped pass

back-heel pass

This skill is useful for switching the play and the angle of attack. With the correct technique the back of the heel can be used to deliver passes either square (to the side) or directly behind. A direct running player will often find a player blocking his path but, with a square pass to a colleague in space, he can take his opponent out of the play. Using the heel to deliver a square pass can be extremely effective as it is more difficult for a defender to read and predict.

A conventional back-heel is a similar technique which can be used when a player finds his path forwards blocked by an opponent. A backheel to a team-mate just behind takes the pressure off and help your team retain possession. Make sure you look before delivery to make sure a team-mate is close enough to reach with a back-heel and that he is not tightly marked.

Former Leeds and Scotland skipper Billy Bremner and his Elland Road team-mate Johnny Giles were great exponents of the heel pass which they used to keep possession to great effect. In the modern game the back-heel is employed in all areas of play – from defence to attack – though it remains a popular skill for midfielders.

4

5

1–2
The attacker's route to goal is blocked by the defender and he has to move across the edge of the 18-yard box.

3
The attacker plays a back-heel pass and keeps his marker at bay by striking the ball with his right foot.

4–5
The ball is played into the path of the on-rushing red player who has a goalscoring opportunity.

40 headed pass   42 swerve pass   44 disguised pass   **46 back-heel pass**   48 chipped pass

1

2

chipped pass

The chip pass is more ambitious than the swerve pass, with the margin for error greater, but when performed correctly can be just as rewarding. Failure to gain enough height on the pass results in an embarrassing pass to an opponent, so it is important to practise this skill and have plenty of confidence before you try it in a match.

The chip can be used in all areas of the field and when used well it is extremely productive - in defence it can be used to clear as an opponent charges in to block; in midfield when being closed down; or in attack when a delicate chip over a defender plays a team-mate in on goal.

The correct way to play a chip is to make a 'stab' at the ball and get your foot right underneath it. Contact is made with the lower part of the instep, not the toe end of the boot, and the idea is to bring the striking foot down sharply and stop quickly to create backspin on the ball which should then loft the ball upwards into the air.

The chip needs only a short back lift and, unlike the swerved pass, little or nothing by way of follow-through.

The aim is to get enough height on the ball to clear the opponent nearest to you so your judgement of distance is as critical as is your technique.

34 wall pass   36 scissors pass   38 power chest pass

3

4

1
Get your body position right and assess the position of the team-mate you are hoping to pass to.

2
'Stab' under the ball in order to get enough loft to clear your opponent.

3–4
The main objective, of course, is not just to lob the ball over the defender but to find your intended target with a well-directed, well-measured pass which is easy to control.

left
Glenn Hoddle leans back and chips the ball over a Manchester City defender in the 1981 FA Cup final replay. The former Spurs midfielder was equally happy to attempt passes over five or 50 yards.

40 headed pass   42 swerve pass   44 disguised pass   46 back-heel pass   **48 chipped pass**

56 bending free-kick   **58** passed free-kick   **60** whipped-in corner   **62** penalties   **64** penalties

long throw

There are effectively two types of throw-in. The short throw designed to keep possession for your team, or the long throw which is used as an attacking measure to put pressure on the opposition defence and create a goalscoring opportunity.

Both types of throw have a place in football. The long throw is a potent attacking weapon, but if over-used it becomes predictable and defenders have a better chance of combating its potential threat. The use of the long throw-in is widespread and many clubs employ a long-throw expert.

The long throw is used anywhere from midway in the opponents' half up to the corner flag and the the thrower's intention is to land the ball somewhere around the penalty spot or six-yard line. A powerful, accurate throw can be very difficult to defend against.

It is not just in recent years that this particular tactic has been employed at professional level, however. In the halcyon days of the 1970s the likes of Chelsea's Ian Hutchinson and Arsenal's John Radford turned the throw-in into something of an art form. Both of these men were tall, well-built strikers but one modern day player has dispelled the myth that you have to be a giant with arms like Arnold Schwarzenegger to be able to produce a long, and legal, throw-in.

Wales midfielder Andy Legg, who has seen service with Swansea, Notts County and Birmingham, weighs in at little more than ten stone and stands at just 5' 7", but until recently was recognised as having the world's longest throw by the *Guinness Book of Records*. In a showdown at Wembley Stadium, Legg recorded a throw of 45.6 metres, although he claims to have thrown well in excess of that in training. So you see, it is more about technique, timing and practice than sheer muscle power.

Tips

The success of a long throw depends both on the length and accuracy of the delivery, in addition to the understanding and awareness of team-mates in the goal-mouth.

i. Keep both feet on the ground when releasing the ball, taking both hands well behind the head. Remember, do not step over the line before you throw the ball.

ii. Concentrate on finding a team-mate and not just hurling the ball as far as you can.

iii. To improve the distance on your throw means developing your technique and practising on a regular basis.

iv. Remember, you throw with your back as well as your arms so try to develop a whiplash movement as you deliver the ball.

v. Get as much power behind the ball as you can by using your fingers as well as your hands and arms. Finally, follow through powerfully with your arms.

1
By arching your back you can use the strength in your upper body as well as your arms. Raise your heels and generate power by pressing with the balls of your feet, but remember to keep your feet on the ground at all times.

2
Being able to throw the ball a long way is one thing, but it is important to know where your team-mates are and to find one of them.

3
Add length to your throw by following through with your arms, giving the ball a final push with your fingers. Stay off the pitch and on your feet until you have released the ball.

4
A team-mate has read your intentions and, using the classic long throw move, now flicks the ball into the danger area for a colleague to attack the goal.

56 bending free-kick   **58** passed free-kick   **60** whipped-in corner   **62** penalties   **64** penalties

flick-up and volley free-kick

Former Coventry City favourites Ernie Hunt and Willie Carr caused a soccer sensation in the 1970s with an astonishing free-kick move which had never been seen before.

In a match against Everton, the pair stood by the ball just outside the penalty area, a wall of yellow-shirted Everton players lined up protecting the goal in front of them. A clever curler around the wall....a powerful drive through it....or perhaps a gentle chip over the top....just what did they have in mind? The answer was something few, if any, had witnessed before. Carr stood over the ball, with a foot either side, facing the touch line while Hunt lined up to take a shot.

On the referee's whistle, ginger-haired Carr squeezed the ball in between his feet and, in one subtle movement, flicked the ball gently into the air inviting Hunt to volley the ball goalwards, which he did with aplomb. Whether the Everton keeper was deceived by the trickery of Carr's move or the power of Hunt's shot is hard to say, but the end result was a spectacular goal which was to be replayed time and time again.

Soon after, Southampton pair Peter Osgood and Jim McAlliog attempted an alternative version. Osgood, stood just outside the penalty area to the right of the goal and provided the subtlety with a gentle flick, scooping the ball into the air while McAlliog ran in to volley home. The nature of the two 'flick and volley' free kicks caused alarm amongst the English Football Association which deemed that such 'trickery', not skill, was unlawful and not in the spirit of the game.

1–3
The player on the ball takes a short free-kick to a team-mate standing in front of him. The receiving player flicks the ball up into the air as his colleague prepares to volley the ball goalwards. The speed of the control and the flick is paramount because the defenders in the wall will try to close down the impending shot.

4–6
The main benefit of this particular free-kick is that the player volleying the ball can strike it so that it clears the wall and dips goalward. It is also possible to generate more power from a volley and the defenders in the wall are left taking evasive action as the ball flies past.

left
England and Southampton forward Matt Le Tissier carefully places the ball before taking a free-kick. Le Tissier is the most recent scorer of a spectacular flick-up and volley free-kick, his goal coming during a League match in 1996.

56 bending free-kick   58 passed free-kick   60 whipped-in corner   62 penalties   64 penalties

bending free-kick

Bending the ball around the wall, with pace, is an art form which is widely associated with the great Brazilians. The likes of Garrincha, Rivelino, Zico and more recently Roberto Carlos have been responsible for some of the most spectacular moments in modern international football.

In recent years, top European stars such as Gianfranco Zola, Thomas Hässler and David Beckham have also proved themselves to be quality exponents of what can no longer be deemed a Samba skill.

However, it is unlikely that we will ever witness a more vicious, curling free kick than the amazing 40-yard 'bender' produced by the brilliant Roberto Carlos in the 1996 Tournoi in France. His incredible, swerving shot in the match between Brazil and Italy seemed to be heading yards wide until it suddenly curled back towards goal so alarmingly that the Italian keeper Peruzzi was powerless to react.

So extraordinary was the strike that a ball boy standing 10-15 yards to the side of the Italian goal was seen to duck out of the way after Carlos had hit the ball, clearly believing the shot was heading wide of the goal and straight towards him.

3

4

Tips

Mastering the art of bending the ball requires not just skill but persistence. Curling the ball does not just happen naturally; to do it properly and effectively takes practice and the will to persevere when it does not come off. The theory is simple enough to understand. Aim the ball wide of the goal, send it around the wall and bring it back far enough to hit the target. In reality, it's not that easy. But here are a few tips to help you on your way.

i. Assess the position of the defensive wall and the goalkeeper and make up your mind where you intend to put the ball. Then stick to it.
ii. You should be looking to place the ball just inside one of the posts, out of the keeper's reach. In order to do this start the ball off about 2–3 feet (one metre) outside the post.
iii. Curling the ball with the inside of the boot (bringing the ball from right to left if you are right-footed) is much easier than using the outside of the boot (bending the ball from left to right if you are right-footed).
iv. To bend the ball from right to left, hit across the right half of the ball rather than striking through the middle of the ball as you would normally.

v. Whip your foot across the ball and exaggerate your follow-through in order to create the spin which will help your shot to curl.

Top tip

Before going for power concentrate on accuracy first. Once you find you are consistently hitting the target with a gentle, curling strike try increasing the pace of the shot and the amount of bend you put on the ball.

1
Assess the position of the wall and the goalkeeper. Place a team-mate on the end of the defensive wall to unsight the keeper further. If you are a left-footed player, like the one shown, you will be looking to curl the ball with the inside of the foot from left back to right, so aim just outside the goalkeeper's far post.
2–4
In addition to putting curl on the ball, you will also need to hit it with pace to get it over or around the keeper and into the net.
left
England players David Beckham (7), Paul Gascoigne (8) and Alan Shearer (9) contemplate a free-kick on the edge of their opponent's penalty area. Each player has his own free-kick speciality, but on this occasion Beckham steps forward to take the kick.

56 bending free-kick   **58** passed free-kick   **60** whipped-in corner   **62** penalties   **64** penalties

passed free-kick

When taking a free-kick just outside the opposition's penalty area, there are a number of options open to an attacking team. We have already talked about the flick-up and volley and the bending free-kick as direct approaches, but there will be times in a game when something other than the straight forward shooting option should be considered.

If the distance from goal is too great, the angle is too acute or there are simply too many defenders in the wall or on the line for you to get in a decent strike, then this is where the passed free-kick comes into play.

You may remember how, during the 1994 World Cup finals, Tomas Brolin scored a classic goal from such a set-play in the match against Romania. Brolin ran over the ball into what appeared an unthreatening position, but made an early run on to the pass, which was played down the side of the wall, and shot past the unsuspecting Romanian keeper.

This type of free-kick depends upon convincing the defending team that you are going to shoot for goal. It's a fair bet, therefore, that you will catch them unawares and not equipped to combat the movement of the attacking players.

1   2   3

1
There are three attacking players involved in the move – the passer, the receiver and the striker. The defenders in the wall believe the taker will go directly for goal.

2
The receiver makes an early run into the box and is picked out by the passer with a low, accurate and firmly struck free-kick.

3
As he does so the striker, who had positioned himself on the edge of the opposition wall, spins away from the static defenders and runs to collect the second pass.

4
With the defence confused the striker finds himself in the clear and with only the keeper to beat.

4

5

56 bending free-kick   **58 passed free-kick**   60 whipped-in corner   62 penalties   64 penalties

whipped-in corner

For a corner kick to be effective the taker not only needs a good technique, he also needs a good idea of what he is trying to achieve. This sounds obvious, but all too often corners are aimlessly swung over, more in hope than expectation, that a team-mate will get to the ball before a defender.

A floated corner hit accurately is fine, but it gives the goalkeeper and defenders a split second longer to react and thwart the potential danger than a ball which is driven in. The 'whipped-in' corner can be hit to either the near or the far post and always creates uncertainty amongst defenders and keepers. It is extremely difficult to defend against because of the pace and lower trajectory of the ball.

If the delivery is good, then even the top defences will have little answer to a driven corner. Manchester United possess two of the best corner experts in world football, England's David Beckham and Wales' Ryan Giggs. One a right-footed player, the other left, they are a permanent menace at corners.

The top players use the inside of the boot, wrapping the foot around the ball, in order to arc it low and hard towards the goal. Notice too how quality players vary their delivery, hitting the near post on a couple of occasions but then whipping the next corner to the far post to confuse the opposition. Italian international Gianfranco Zola is lethal from this dead ball situation. And the diminutive striker is able to deliver clinical corners with either foot and with equal effect.

52 long throw   **54** flick-up and volley free-kick

Tips

i. A poorly delivered corner is frustrating for everyone. Take your time and hit a quality ball.
ii. Assess the position of your team-mates and decide who you are going to pick out. Know when and where they are going to run.
iii. Strike the ball with pace, and a touch of bend, to make it difficult to defend against.

1

The corner taker has lined himself up so that he can 'whip' the ball around the defender and towards the goal. The ball is struck firmly and positively, bending slightly from right to left.

2-4

Keep the ball away from the keeper and give your team-mates the best possible chance to meet the ball before a defender.

left

A good delivery must be combined with aerial ability for corners to be effective. Ruud Gullit, seen here playing for Sampdoria, was regarded as one of the best headers in world football. On this occasion Gullit gets above the Roma defence to head down and goalwards.

side-foot penalty

Taking a penalty on the training ground is a piece of cake. But, when a player is asked to take a crucial spot kick in a tense match situation, that's a different matter entirely.

At times like that it's not just about technique or having the ability to strike a ball cleanly, it's about concentration and nerve. When nerves set in and doubts creep into the mind, a player's technique goes askew.

The introduction of penalty shoot-outs in cup competitions has meant even more drama, more tension and more fall guys. The worst crime of all when taking penalties is not hitting the target at all. Rule number one is at least force the keeper to make a save. Roberto Baggio famously failed to achieve this in the final of the 1994 World Cup when he struck his penalty over the bar.

Rule number two is make up your mind where you are going to put the ball – and don't change it! After that, it's just a case of hitting the ball well and accurately. Simple.

Most players prefer the placed penalty, putting more emphasis on accuracy than power. Eric Cantona, one of the coolest customers in the game, always liked to stroke the ball into the corner. However, Dutch international sweeper Ronald Koeman, for example, often favoured a less subtle approach. As with his trademark free-kicks, Koeman relied on power rather than placement to beat goalkeepers and, more often than not, it worked.

1

2

52 long throw   **54** flick-up and volley free-kick

Tips

i. When you have decided where to put your penalty, do not change your mind on your run up. The results can be woeful.

ii. Look at the goal before you take the kick, but look at the ball when striking. Keep your head down to avoid 'skying' the ball.

iii. If you are going for accuracy rather than power then make sure you place the ball as near to the post as possible.

iv. Be positive and focused.

Top tip

Do not look at the goalkeeper as you take the penalty because he will do anything he can to put you off.

1–4

The side-foot penalty high to the keeper's right or left-hand side is the most common and, over the years, the most effective. Concentrate on hitting the ball cleanly and positively towards the selected corner, using the side of your strongest foot as shown.

A–C

Sending the keeper the wrong way by deceiving him on the run-up can be an effective tactic. Shape to hit the ball in one direction and glance at the corner you want the keeper to dive toward. This approach can be risky so plenty of practice is recommended.

4

56 bending free-kick   **58** passed free-kick   **60** whipped-in corner   **62 penalties**   **64** penalties

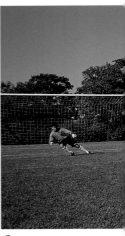

1   2   3

chipped penalty

A penalty is a keeper's best chance to become a hero, so you can be sure that he'll make every effort to pull off a save. In most cases, keepers are so keen that they move early and dive, full-stretch, in one direction or the other. To the coolest of strikers, this gives the opportunity to score with one of the cheekiest moves in the game – the chipped penalty. As the keeper dives, the striker just chips the ball straight into the middle of the goal and over the diving keeper. Couldn't be more simple.

Trinidad and Tobago striker Dwight Yorke used this penalty to great effect in a Cup game for Aston Villa. The pacy forward dinked the ball over the opposing keeper to score the game's deciding goal. On this occasion the accolades came thick and fast. However the danger with this technique is that if the goalkeeper stands up in the middle of his goal he can easily catch the ball and make the striker look a fool.

The clearest example of a chipped penalty failing came in an international friendly between England and Brazil in 1992. Striker Gary Lineker was England's nominated penalty taker and in goal for Brazil that day was Taffarel. Lineker, scorer of two penalties in the World Cup quarter-final against Cameroon in 1990, elected to try and chip Taffarel, but the South American keeper read his intentions and had time to adjust his footing and catch the ball. Lineker was left ruing the missed chance – if he had scored he would have equalled Bobby Charlton's all-time England scoring record.

52 long throw   54 flick-up and volley free-kick

4

5

Confidence is everything. As with all penalties never change your mind on the run up.

1
Try to deceive the keeper by looking toward the corner of the goal.

2
Watch the keeper's position on your run-up – he should start to move. Look at the ball as you strike it.

3
Stab at the ball and don't follow through.

4–5
The keeper dives out of the way and the ball nestles in the net.

left
Dwight Yorke elects to chip the ball over Sheffield United keeper Alan Kelly. On this occasion the striker gets his technique right and lifts the ball over the diving keeper to score the only goal of the game.

BEATING YOUR MAN
68 the dummy   **70** step-over   **72** drag back

74 Cruyff turn   **76** Beardsley feint   **78** stop start   **80** nutmeg   **82** round the corner   **84** rolling foot over ball

1

2

the dummy

There have been few better dribblers of the ball, in the history of the game, than the legendary Stanley Matthews. Even George Best, a mesmeric runner with the ball himself, would admit Matthews was the master in this department, the original 'Wizard of the Dribble' as he was dubbed until he retired at the incredible age of 50.

Sir Stan, as he is now affectionately known, enjoyed a 30-year playing career with Blackpool and Stoke City. It was with Blackpool that Matthews won the FA Cup after an epic battle with Bolton in 1953. His performance was so impressive that the match was dubbed 'The Matthews Final'. The great man also has a classic football move named after him. The 'dummy', 'shimmy', or 'feint' is more popularly known as 'The Matthews'.

Defenders in the 1950s knew all about the skills of the magical Matthews, especially the feint or dummy he used so many times to beat opponents. Perhaps they knew what he was about to do, but few managed to stop him. Matthews' trickery, ability to change direction, his control and pace meant he was unstoppable on his day.

4

Top tip

To make the most of the feint, you need to over-emphasise your first movement to force your opponent off balance. Watch how top players exaggerate the movement.

1

The defender has put the attacker in a difficult position as he has successfully closed down the space. The attacker feints to go to his left, by dropping the shoulder as shown.

2

The defender is now committed to going to the attacker's left and as he does so, the forward dramatically changes direction, going back to the right and taking the ball with the outside of his right foot.

3–4

From the crouched position shown, the attacker knocks the ball away from his opponent (not too far) and sprints away from him. By the time the defender has recovered his balance, the attacker will be past him.

left

Stanley Matthews glides down the wing without a defender in sight. The dummy was his trademark – on this occasion, as so often, Matthews had no doubt tricked his way past all those who stood between him and goal.

74 Cruyff turn   76 Beardsley feint   78 stop start   80 nutmeg   82 round the corner   84 rolling foot over ball

step-over

There are two types of step-over which have proved both popular and effective in the modern game. The first requires the use of just one foot and is a step over the ball from outside to in, followed by a flick away using the outside of the same foot.

The step-over illustrated here is for players who are both confident and competent with both feet as it requires a right foot approach, followed by a left foot take away (or vice versa).

This is a tried and trusted trick for forwards like the Brazilian Juninho and the Dutchman Marc Overmars. The move requires balance, deception and a swift change of direction. The idea is to make the defender believe that you are intending to take him on down the right-hand side (his left), but by stepping over and round the ball from inside to out you have provided yourself with the opportunity to take the ball away with your left foot down the defender's right-hand side. The defender is thrown off balance thus giving you vital seconds in which to get away.

1
As the attacker approaches, the defender sees that he is moving the ball with the outside of his right foot. The defender assumes his opponent intends to take him on around the outside.

2
Instead of knocking the ball past the defender with the outside of his right foot, the player runs the same foot around the front of the ball in a circular motion from inside to out. Note the defender moves towards his left.

3
The right foot is outside the ball and slightly forward of it to enable the player to bring his left foot across for the take away.

4
By quickly adjusting his feet, the attacker's right foot is now wide of the ball and his left is inside ready to knock it away with the outside of the boot.

5
The defender is committed to going to his left, but the forward has changed his direction of attack and is away from his marker.

1

2

3

4

5

74 Cruyff turn   76 Beardsley feint   78 stop start   80 nutmeg   82 round the corner   84 rolling foot over ball

the drag back

Whenever there's a debate about 'who's the greatest footballer ever?' you can guarantee that the name of George Best will crop up at some point. Many would say Best was 'the' best. He was quite simply a genius and arguably the most naturally talented player the British Isles has ever produced.

While Best's chequered playing career was cut short, ultimately, by the player's addiction to the high life, the contribution he made during the late 1960s and early 1970s was immeasurable. Beautifully balanced, lightning quick, brave, he had more tricks than anyone of that era had seen before. Best was a wonderful sight for spectators; a nightmare vision for defenders.

A European Cup winner in 1968, he probably never scaled the heights his talents warranted but George Best brought pleasure to millions...and still does. Most attacking players have a couple of tricks up their sleeve. Best had an absolute sackful, including the drag back which was cleverly designed to tease and torment embarrassed opponents. He would cheekily show the ball to his opponents as he ran towards them and, just as they were about to make a tackle, he would drag the ball back with the sole of his boot before pushing the ball away again in one graceful movement. Even if his opponents knew what Best was intending to do, they were powerless to stop him.

1
The attacker 'shows' the ball to his opponent as he approaches and the defender prepares to make his tackle.

2
As the defender dives in, the attacker puts his foot on the ball and prepares to drag it back towards his own body.

3
The body is perfectly balanced as the attacker rolls the ball back using the sole of his boot. Already he is preparing to use the same foot to push the ball away. The player has turned his foot square to the ball and is in position to go past the defender on the outside as his opponent's momentum continues to take him the other way.

4
The defender is committed to his tackle and the attacker is in the clear.

the double drag back

Dutch master Dennis Bergkamp used this skill to glorious effect in scoring a wonder goal for Arsenal in 1997. Faced with a tight situation and defenders all around him, Bergkamp picked up a loose ball. With his first touch he dragged it back away from goal with the sole of his left foot, he then spun round on the ball with his right foot, dragging it back at right angles and made a diagonal run for the Sunderland goal. Bergkamp finished the move with a delicate chip over the Sunderland keeper.

A

Start the move by putting your right foot on the ball.

B

Twist through 90 degrees as you prepare to put your left foot on the ball.

C

The left foot then replaces the right on the top of the ball.

D

You then rotate through another 90 degrees and take the ball away.

Top tip

One foot or the other should be in contact with the ball throughout this manoeuvre which requires excellent balance....and, of course, practice.

74 Cruyff turn   76 Beardsley feint   78 stop start   80 nutmeg   82 round the corner   84 rolling foot over ball

the Cruyff turn

Football in the 1970s was all about skill and entertainment. Winning, of course, was important, but this was a decade dominated by gifted individuals, great characters, who delighted and excited fans the world over with their unique genius.

Franz Beckenbauer, George Best, Jairzinho and Pele were all household names, but it was the Dutchman Johan Cruyff who was the real symbol of this era of 'fantasy football', a beautifully balanced player whose repertoire of skills was breathtaking.

The 'total football' approach of the Dutch national team around the time of the 1974 World Cup finals (Holland ultimately lost to West Germany in a classic final) caught the imagination of people inside and outside the sport alike.

Cruyff was the captain and the team's inspiration, displaying outrageous skills and wonderful vision – all undertaken with the utmost grace and finesse; all designed to bamboozle even the smartest defenders. One of the many moves he perfected – in addition to his ability to score wonderful goals – still

carries his name today.....the Cruyff turn.

If you get it right, the Cruyff turn will allow you to beat a defender and open up space to move into, throwing your opponent completely out the game in the process. Get it wrong, and you will invariably lose possession for your team – and probably fall flat on your face in doing so – which is why it should only be used in attacking areas....not on the edge of your penalty area.

Cruyff mastered the art and many players have done so since. Few better in recent times than England's Paul Gascoigne who performed the perfect Cruyff turn to beat two opponents during his inspirational 1990 World Cup performance – against Holland!

Most players can only turn one way (usually to the right in the case of right-footed players). Practise turning both ways – you'll be a nightmare for defenders to mark if you can perfect it. The key to the turn is to convince your marker that you are going to play the ball forwards to go past him on the outside. Your body position should make him think that is what you are going to do but then, at the last moment, sell him the dummy.

3

4

Top tip

*Don't become predictable by trying to use the
Cruyff turn too often in a game. Your move
will become easy to read. Keep defenders
guessing by using it sparingly and when the
need arises.*

1

The Cruyff turn is all about deception. Here the
player is making the defender believe he wants to go
past him on the outside and perhaps produce a
cross, or shot, with his right foot....

2–3

....but instead of taking the ball on, he stops quickly
in his tracks and takes his right foot around the side
of the ball, knocking it behind his standing foot as
shown.

4

Having flicked the ball inside the defender with the
inside of his right foot, the player turns sharply away
from his opponent, who is still committed to his forward motion.

left

Dutch captain Johan Cruyff demonstrates his exceptional control and balance to trick his way past an
Argentina defender.

74 Cruyff turn   76 Beardsley feint   78 stop start   80 nutmeg   82 round the corner   84 rolling foot over ball

1

2

68 the dummy   **70** step-over   **72** drag back

the Beardsley feint

Peter Beardsley has long been recognised among footballers as the ultimate professional. Strange that he was allowed to leave Manchester United without playing a game following a £200,000 move from Vancouver Whitecaps. But United's loss was their rivals' gain and Beardsley went on to make a mockery of the Old Trafford club's decision. In a glorious career with Carlisle, Newcastle, Liverpool, Everton and Bolton, Beardsley has established a reputation as a player who puts maximum effort into both his training and his playing. More than 50 England caps were a just reward for the inventive forward who was never frightened to experiment and who perfected many individual moves, including the move shown here.

Beardsley is an extremely fleet-footed player and late in his career he was still twisting and turning defenders inside out with the deception and speed of his moves.

1–2

As you run towards your opponent with the ball on your right foot make out you are going to take the ball away with your left foot.

3–4

Really exaggerate the movement of the left leg and the feint before taking the ball off to your left with the right foot. When done at speed this is highly effective – just ask Beardsley's bewildered opponents.

left

Wanderer in full flight: Beardsley leads a Bolton attack during the 1996–97 season.

3

4

74 Cruyff turn   **76 Beardsley feint**   78 stop start   80 nutmeg   82 round the corner   84 rolling foot over ball

the stop start

Many words have been used to describe the complex character and talent of Paul Gascoigne. From 'world beater' to 'daft as a brush', more column inches of tabloid newspapers and magazine articles have been devoted to him than any other modern day football player. But while his attitude and application have often been called into question, one thing that's never been queried is his unique talent.

When his mind is right and his fitness level up to scratch there are few midfielders in the world who compare to him. Impeccable touch, great balance, wonderful ability to run with the ball and beat defenders, power and aggression all combined with a striker's instinct to score goals. He also has a massive repertoire of individual skills which he has the supreme confidence to carry out under any circumstances.

During Italia 90 he gave a perfect demonstration of the Cruyff turn against Holland and against Scotland in Euro 96 he flicked the ball impudently over Colin Hendry before firing in a sweet volley. Both these and more are in the Gascoigne catalogue, like this cheeky move he's made virtually his own....

When Gascoigne performs this skill he makes it look so simple you wonder why more players don't do it. The truth is that it's more difficult than it looks because it requires a deftness of touch few players are blessed with. It must be carried out while the player is in full flow and with such speed of foot, which merely adds to the difficulty. Ideal on the edge of your opponents' penalty area where a change of pace can get you past an opponent and into space in the box.

1

When running with the ball prior to carrying out this skill it is important to have your eyes on the ball, not the man you are looking to beat.

2

Bring your right foot up and over the ball with the standing foot close behind.

3

Place your right foot down on top of the ball with a minimum of force. Do not stamp on it. Your opponent now thinks you are bringing body and ball to a halt, but with your right foot still resting gently on the ball bring your left foot forward to meet it.

4

Release the pressure with the right foot and poke the ball forward with your left foot in a quick, jumping movement. The stop-start manoeuvre will confuse the defender and give you an extra yard on him.

left

The perfect stop start move. Gascoigne removes his left foot from the top of the ball and simultaneously strikes the ball with his right foot.

1   2   3   4

74 Cruyff turn   76 Beardsley feint   **78 stop start**   80 nutmeg   82 round the corner   84 rolling foot over ball

1

2

68 the dummy   **70** step-over   **72** drag back

the nutmeg

One of the most embarrassing things to happen to a player on the field – outside scoring an own goal or missing an open one – is falling victim to the dreaded nutmeg. For the player 'nutting' an opponent (the art of pushing the ball through his legs and gleefully running around him) the feeling of satisfaction when it comes off is almost as great as scoring a goal. For the open-stanced, red-faced opponent it is a nightmare which will continue long after the game has finished as even his closest pals take great delight in reminding him of the incident.

The simple answer, of course, is to keep your legs shut when an opponent is running toward you. In reality, it's not as easy as that. For starters, if your legs are together you are not well balanced and, worse still, not well positioned to push off in one direction or another. Keep your legs open, but not to the extent of inviting the player to take advantage with 'a meg'.

For the player in possession there are, invariably, better options available than the gamble of losing possession by trying to poke the ball through an opponent's legs. More nutmegs fail than succeed. But to many players it's an irresistible challenge and the rewards are immense.

Top tip
Throughout the move it is important to smile at all times and, remember, no nutmeg is complete without the customary cry of 'NUTS' as you round the embarrassed opponent to collect the ball.

1
As the player in possession approaches the defender he quickly recognises the opportunity to nutmeg his open-legged opponent.

2
Decide what are you are going to do and choose the right moment to carry out the move.

3
When you consider the gap between your opponents legs to be wide enough to get the ball successfully through, go for it!

4
As soon as you've knocked the ball through his legs (not with any great force, mind) run round him to collect it. If your opponent is moving to the left you go to the right, and vice versa.

74 Cruyff turn   76 Beardsley feint   78 stop start   **80 nutmeg**   82 round the corner   84 rolling foot over ball

round the corner

This is probably a phrase few readers have come across before, but it is a genuine name for a rarely used skill. Clever players with a subtle touch and space – people like the Brazilian Juninho and Alessandro Del Piero of Italy – are more likely to be suited to this move than bigger, less mobile players.

Awareness of what is going on around you, especially in the space that you are hoping to run into behind your opponent, is vital. The ideal time to attempt this skill is when you have your back to goal with a defender in close attention. The opponent is probably thinking, as the pass comes into your feet, that you will hold the ball up to pass to a team-mate or that you will try to turn with the ball in order to take him on in a one-against-one situation. What he will not be expecting is for you to try and beat him 'round the corner' in the fashion illustrated.

The Brazilian Juninho is such a busy, industrious player that he is very difficult to mark at the best of times. The little midfield wizard, who was such a hit with Middlesbrough fans during his brief stay on Teesside, is always on the move, always looking to create something out of nothing with his fleetness of foot. His ability to twist and turn from tight situations at speed makes him a slippery character to deal with. And it is that ability to turn away from an unsuspecting opponent at the bat of an eyelid which makes him perfectly equipped to carry out this 'round the corner' skill.

1
As the ball is played into you, be aware of the position of your opponent and the space behind him which you are planning to run into.

2–3
As your opponent moves in, lean to the left and look to get the slightest of touches with the outside of your right foot. Notice how the player is looking to graze the outside of his boot down the inside of the ball.

4
If your flick is subtle enough it will cause the ball to lift gently and spin past the static defender. You begin your move around the other side of him. By twisting and turning to the left you can go round your defender with ease and collect the ball.

68 the dummy   70 step-over   72 drag back

74 Cruyff turn   76 Beardsley feint   78 stop start   80 nutmeg   **82 round the corner**   84 rolling foot over ball

68 the dummy   **70** step-over   **72** drag back

rolling foot over ball

A defender who won't commit himself and instead stands up and waits for you to make the first move can be a difficult proposition. The best way to get past your stubborn marker is to force him to make a challenge. One of the many ways you can trick an opponent into committing himself is to roll your foot over the ball. This is a simple skill but it can be effective if you get your technique right.

As you approach the defender you must try to deceive him into thinking that you are going to knock the ball past him. Draw your leg back as if to make a full contact with the ball, but slow your swing down as you bring your foot toward the ball. Instead of making a full contact with the ball, just lightly roll your foot over the top of the ball. The defender should commit himself and you will be able to change direction and move into the space that has opened up. The stubborn marker is now rooted to the spot and in no position to pursue you.

This skill is often employed by tricky midfielders like David Ginola and Zvonimir Boban. It can also be used to force goalkeepers to go to ground in one-against-one situatons (see page 108).

1
The defender in white stays on his feet as the attacker in red approaches. The striker decides to try and commit the defender and shapes as if to knock the ball to the defender's left using the outside of his right foot.

2
The attacker brings his foot down to the ball and, instead of striking it, rolls his foot over the top of the ball. The defender plants his left foot forward to make a challenge.

3
The attacker rolls the ball to his left and away from the, now committed, defender and moves into space. The defender is left rooted to the spot.

left
Brazilian Juninho is a defender's nightmare. The diminutive forward combines both exceptional control and a low centre of gravity which help him trick his way out of tight situations and past opponents.

74 Cruyff turn   76 Beardsley feint   78 stop start   80 nutmeg   82 round the corner   **84 rolling foot over ball**

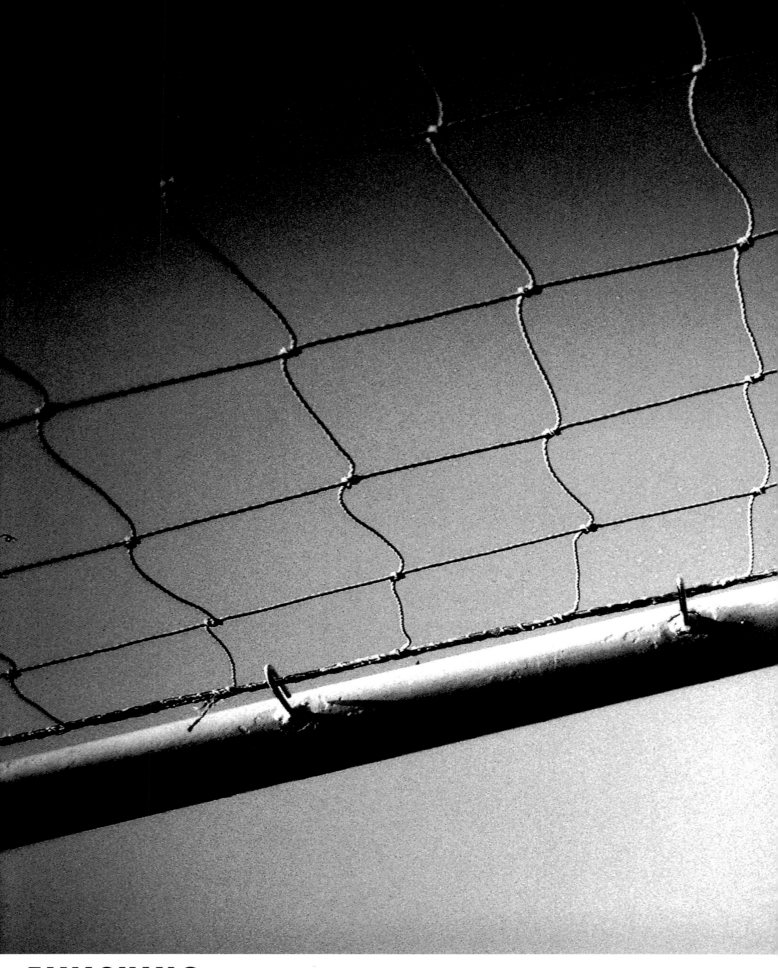

FINISHING   **88** volleying   **90** chip   **92** overhead kick   **94** scissors kick   **96** diving header

98 scoop   **100** swerve   **102** glancing header   **104** power shooting   **106** sending keeper down   **108** rounding keeper

volleying

The volley is a precise skill which, when mastered, can produce explosive and spectacular results. There is no margin for error when trying to strike the ball while it is in the air and if you get it wrong the results can be embarrassing. Timing, co-ordination, balance and body position are all essential to this most difficult skill.

There have been a number of great players down the years who have reaped the benefits of perfecting their volleying technique.

Former Manchester United legend Bobby Charlton, still England's record goalscorer, had a reputation as one of the game's great master-blasters. Few players in the history of the sport can have scored so many spectacular, long range goals – a large portion courtesy of the volley.

Obtaining both power and accuracy is extremely difficult, but Charlton and many others since, have benefited from hours of training ground practice. Marco Van Basten, formerly of AC Milan and Holland, was a wonderfully balanced player with exquisite technique – as he demonstrated with devastating effect in the 1988 European Championship final. Van Basten sealed victory for Holland over the USSR with one of the most remarkable volleyed goals of the modern era. From an awkward angle, the Dutch master struck Arnold Muhren's 60-yard, crossfield pass first time past the stunned figure of Rinat Dasaev in the Soviet goal.

Van Basten's timing and technique is similar to that of Italian star Gianluca Vialli, whose skills have illuminated European football for many years. He too has scored wonderful goals with venomous volleys during a distinguished career which has won him many medals and admirers.

1
Note the body position as the player addresses the ball and uses his outstretched arms to aid balance.

2
The player's eyes are permanently fixed on the ball, not the goal, and his head is over the ball in order to keep the shot down.

3
Using the front of the boot, the player strikes the ball with the 'sweet spot' to gain maximum power.

4
The benefit of keeping the head over the ball is shown in this picture as the player follows through rather than stabs at the ball.

Top tip
As with a golf shot, power can be generated by the timing of your strike rather than the amount of force you put into it.

98 scoop   **100** swerve   **102** glancing header   **104** power shooting   **106** sending keeper down   **108** rounding keeper

the chip

A delicate chip over a six-foot keeper is a dream for a striker; a nightmare for a goalie. Just ask Scotland keeper Neil Sullivan. The unfortunate Wimbledon player was beaten with two inch-perfect lobs within weeks of the start of the 1996–97 season. The most spectacular of these goals was a 50-yard lob from Manchester United's David Beckham. Real Zaragoza midfielder Nayim also scored a notable lob over Arsenal keeper David Seaman in the final of the European Cup Winners' Cup in 1995. This goal was all the more spectacular as it came in the final minute of extra time.

Timing is at the essence of lobbing or chipping a keeper. If you delay your effort too long the keeper will get back in time to catch the ball as it tamely drops goalward. So weigh up your options and if the lob is on, with the keeper off his line, take your chance. Without awareness and vision you will never be able to perfect this skill.

BASIC TECHNIQUE

To get the ball into the air, you will need to strike underneath it using a stabbing motion. Lean back as you strike the ball and don't follow through. Practise so that you are able to vary the height and distance of the lob.

1
The player prepares to lob or chip the ball using the instep having spotted the keeper off his line.

2
Like a golfer with a lofted club, he chips the ball goalwards using a stabbing motion in order to gain instant height.

3
The player's strike is perfect and has enough height, and weight, to carry over the stranded goalkeeper. Concentrate on getting the right amount of pace and height on the ball so that it clears the keeper and also drops beneath the crossbar into an empty net.

Top tip

Check the positioning of the keeper early on in the game. If he likes to stray to the edge of his 18-yard box when the ball is in the midfield you may able to lob him.

below, left
David Beckham chips the ball from the halfway-line to score during Manchester United's opening fixture of the 1996–97 season at Wimbledon. Even though the ball travelled more than 50 yards, Beckham has merely stabbed at it with a minimum of follow-through.

98 scoop   **100** swerve   **102** glancing header   **104** power shooting   **106** sending keeper down   **108** rounding keeper

1

2

overhead kick

There's no more exhilarating sight in football than an athletic player scoring with an acrobatic overhead kick. Such moments of improvisation are rare and are guaranteed to bring even the most conservative fans to their feet in appreciation.

Few, if any, players in recent years have scored so many goals in this unorthodox fashion as Mexican Hugo Sanchez. The former Real Madrid idol was not the tallest of strikers yet was able to launch himself to incredible heights to produce a plethora of incredible goals. The celebrations which always followed – an acrobatic somersault and back flip – also became one of his elaborate trademarks.

Former Manchester United and Scotland striker Denis Law was equally adept at producing the unexpected. Law's quick-witted nature, his athleticism and his fantastic skill made him a cult hero at Old Trafford, even amongst such exalted company as Best and Charlton. It was only the curious decision of an over-officious referee which robbed Law of a great goal in the 1967 Charity Shield clash with Spurs. Spinning beneath a cross lofted in from the left wing, the Scottish showman stretched every muscle to propel himself upwards before driving the ball home with the most outrageous of overheads. There was a moment's silence before the crowd erupted. The fans had been used to seeing Law's dazzling artistry, but this was special. Sadly, the goal was ruled out by the referee and erased from the record books, if not the memories of those who witnessed it.

Top tip

Attempting to kick the ball when it is at head height or above can be deemed dangerous play if opponents are close, so awareness of their position is vital.

WARNING

Overhead kicks can also be extremely dangerous to the kicker. Never use this skill on hard surfaces such as concrete or astro turf. If possible, practise using a soft crash mat to cushion your fall.

1

The leap is initiated by the non-kicking foot and you can see how the player is already beginning to lean away from the ball. Note the position of the arms.

2

The non-kicking leg is now up to waist height while the kicking foot remains on the ground. Again the arms are positioned to provide balance while the back is arched further.

3

With the body almost parallel to the ground the kicking leg now swings into action, arcing towards the ball. Note how the player's eyes have never once left the ball. The kick is completed when the kicking leg makes contact with the ball which is propelled over the head towards goal. The arms are now brought down to help cushion the fall to ground.

right

Flying Frenchman. David Ginola keeps his eye on the ball and uses his athleticism to deliver a perfect overhead kick.

88 volleying   90 chip   **92 overhead kick**   94 scissors kick   96 diving header

3

98 scoop   **100** swerve   **102** glancing header   **104** power shooting   **106** sending keeper down   **108** rounding keeper

scissors kick

This skill is similar in many ways to the of the overhead kick. It is used to strike balls played at between knee and shoulder height and gets its name because the legs cross quickly, as the player is in mid-air, in a scissors motion.

German international Jürgen Klinsmann is one of the best exponents of this skill. Such is his athleticism that he has used the scissors movement even when the ball is above head height. With perfect technique and a lightning quick switch of the legs in mid-air, he gains both power and accuracy in sensational style.

Klinsmann, whose medal-laden career took him to Germany, Italy, France and England, has scored many great goals, but one of the most spectacular came in an English league match against Everton. The ball was played above shoulder height to Klinsmann and the scissors kick did not look possible, but with a whiplash-type movement he generated such power that Neville Southall in the Everton goal could hardly have seen the ball let alone do anything to prevent it bulging the net behind.

DANGEROUS PLAY
Like the overhead kick, the scissors is often deemed dangerous by officials so it's important to make sure you have enough room to carry out this skill safely.

1

2

88 volleying   90 chip   92 overhead kick   **94 scissors kick**   96 diving header

1
The player is side-on to the goal and facing the cross, which is coming towards him from the right wing. The left arm is already out for balance and the player is on his toes ready to leap into action.

2
Leaning back slightly and with arms outstretched the player now assesses the height of the cross and the kicking leg is pulled back ready for the strike.

3
As contact is made with the ball the non-kicking leg leaves the ground and the player is airborne as the kicking foot swings round to face the goal.

4
By spinning round in the air the player's body now faces the goal.

left
In 1978 and 1979 Kevin Keegan was voted European Footballer of the Year. These awards were recognition for a player who combined considerable skill with an unrivalled work-rate. Never a player to avoid a ball played at an awkward height, Keegan is shown here in mid-air having delivered a perfect scissors kick.

98 scoop   **100** swerve   **102** glancing header   **104** power shooting   **106** sending keeper down   **108** rounding keeper

Not only must you possess good heading technique and agility for this skill, you must also be as brave as a lion. Diving low to head the ball in a crowded penalty area means you run the risk of getting a kick in the face.

Putting your head where the boots are flying is not always advisable, but a goal which comes from such a show of courage gives a gutsy striker incredible satisfaction. Jürgen Klinsmann is one striker who is agile and brave enough to score some wonderful goals in this manner. Two of Klinsmann's international predecessors, Gerd Müller and Karl-Heinz Rummenigge, were also not averse to diving headlong to connect with a team-mate's cross.

Both Rummenigge and Müller were lucky enough to play and score in World Cup finals – Müller scoring the winner in 1970 and Rummenigge heading in a Brehme corner as Argentina defeated West Germany in 1986. These prolific strikers were so keen to add to their goals tally that they were happy to throw themselves at the ball whatever the danger.

Few British players in recent times have displayed more courage than the former Scotland striker Andy Gray. Throughout a long career with Aston Villa, Wolves and Everton in England's top division, Gray took bravery to the extreme and received a number of painful blows as a result. But he always bounced back and was still throwing himself about in horizontal fashion at the twilight of his career. Everton fans will recall one particular goal, which Gray scored in his customary 'dive bomb' style, in a classic victory over Sunderland during the Goodison club's Championship-winning season of 1987. The crowd rose to acclaim their idol as he bravely converted a low cross from Peter Reid with a powerful header from within a crowded six-yard box.

CHOOSE YOUR MOMENT
The diving header is used when the ball arrives at between shoulder and knee height. The other option for balls played at this height is the scissors kick; however this offers less control than the header. Different situations call for different techniques, and while it may be worth diving in amongst the boots to head a winner in a World Cup final, sticking your neck out in a practice match may not be worth the risk.

diving header

88 volleying   90 chip   92 overhead kick   94 scissors kick   **96 diving header**

1
The player is using his left leg to project himself forward towards the ball played from the wing, which is coming at below head height.

2
Both feet are in the air and the player is virtually horizontal to the ground in classic diving header style, with the forehead making powerful contact with the ball.

3–4
The player literally launches himself at the ball to gain extra power, twisting the head to direct the ball goalwards and putting the arms out to protect his fall.

Top tip
Even though you are putting your head in amongst the flying feet and probably don't wish to see what's coming, you must keep your eyes open and firmly fixed on the ball at all times. A whack in the face is going to hurt whether you see it coming or not and, once you've committed yourself to the dive, there's no way out.

98 scoop   **100** swerve   **102** glancing header   **104** power shooting   **106** sending keeper down   **108** rounding keeper

1

2

the scoop

Only a player with supreme confidence, and more than a touch of arrogance, would attempt this particular form of finishing. There are more conventional ways of beating a keeper in a 'one-against-one' situation, but this is a guaranteed crowd pleaser....if it comes off, that is!

Goals scored as a result of 'the scoop' are few and far between. However football fans were treated to the most audacious of scoops in the quarter-finals of the European Championships in 1996. In a game of few chances, the Czech Republic winger Karel Poborsky caught the Portugal keeper Vitor Baia completely by surprise as he flicked the ball over him and into the net from the edge of the 18-yard box. Poborsky's goal was all the more notable as he scooped a moving ball while running toward goal – most players would only attempt this most difficult skill from a static position.

TO SCOOP OR TO CHIP

The scoop and the chip have the same aim; to get the ball over a keeper who is off of his line and down quickly enough to fall under the bar and into the net. The chip can be used when shooting from as far out as the halfway line, but it is difficult to get the ball to come down quickly enough when you are in the 18-yard box. From close in on goal the scoop is a more useful skill as it is possible to loop the ball over a standing keeper from inside the penalty area. Both of these techniques require a high level of skill and therefore a great deal of practice.

88 volleying   90 chip   92 overhead kick   94 scissors kick   96 diving header

3

Tips

i. Position your standing foot beside the ball.
ii. Lean back as you make contact with the bottom of the ball.
iii. Don't try to strike the ball too hard.
iv. Make a full follow-through and concentrate on maintaining your balance.
v. Take the wind into account. This skill is of limited value when playing into a strong wind, though with the wind behind you it can be extremely productive.
vi. Practise this skill on the training ground. Try varying your follow-through to change the pace and height of your scoops.

1
As the keeper comes off his line, the striker prepares to scoop the ball. It is important to check your stride before connecting with the ball.

2
To perform 'the scoop' you must follow through with your striking foot as shown.

3
Clearing the keeper is one thing, but the scoop needs to be controlled for the ball to drop under the bar.

left
Karel Poborsky lets flie with his famous scoop shot in the quarter-final of Euro 96 against Portugal. Note the Czech striker's follow-through position.

98 scoop   100 swerve   102 glancing header   104 power shooting   106 sending keeper down   108 rounding keeper

swerve shot

The art of bending the ball around a wall at free-kicks is explained on page 56 and the same principles apply when attempting a curler in open play. Because you are running at speed with a defender perhaps no more than a yard away – as opposed to ten yards at a free-kick – it is logical to assume that bending a moving ball is more difficult than doing so from a dead-ball situation. However, many players are more confident striking a ball on the run and feel they can get more 'bend' on the ball than they can from a static position.

Your first thought when attempting a curling shot is the position of the goalkeeper and the point of the goal you are looking to hit. Usually when a player is trying to bend a ball in this way the inside of the far post is his target – although strikers often catch keepers off guard by curling the ball towards the near post. If you're attempting the former, you should be looking to aim the ball wide of the

goal, hitting around the closest defender, in order to try and curl it back inside the far post but out of the keeper's reach.

In order to do this start the ball off about 2–3 feet (one metre) outside the post, curling the ball with the inside of the boot, bringing it from right to left if you are right-footed or from left to right if you are left-footed. It is important to hit the ball with pace, as well as spin, so that the keeper has less time to get across his goal and make a save. A fraction of a second is critical in these situations.

Many great goals have been scored in this way and of the current crop of world stars, players such as Ryan Giggs, Gianfranco Zola and Zinedine Zidane lead the way. Zidane, in particular, has wonderful power, balance and technique which enables him to bend the ball from seemingly impossible positions, as he has shown on numerous occasions for both France and Juventus.

1

2

88 volleying   90 chip   92 overhead kick   94 scissors kick   96 diving header

1

By positioning your body square on to the ball and almost parallel to the goal you have a better chance of 'wrapping' your striking foot around the ball with the inside of the boot.

2

To bend the ball from left to right hit across the left half of the ball rather than striking through the middle as you would normally. Set the ball wide of the goal, away from the nearest opponent.

3

Notice how the player's body has moved around by well over 90 degrees from its original position. This has been caused by the follow-through which is essential to get extra curl on the ball.

4

The ball has come back from outside the goal and out of the reach of the diving goalkeeper.

98 scoop   **100 swerve**   102 glancing header   104 power shooting   106 sending keeper down   108 rounding keeper

glancing header

1

2

88 volleying   **90** chip   **92** overhead kick   **94** scissors kick   **96** diving header

It was, and still remains, the greatest night enjoyed by an English club side in European competition. Manchester United were crowned champions of Europe – the first team from this country to achieve such status. A magnificent 4–1 victory over the mighty Benfica, Eusebio and all, was inspired by Bobby Charlton, who scored two goals on a never-to-be forgotten night at Wembley Stadium. Charlton was more renowned for his powerful shooting and long-range goals than his heading ability, yet it was the head of the United legend which set the Red Devils on the road to victory. The United skipper rose majestically to meet an in-swinging cross from full-back Tony Dunne and his fabulous, glancing header gave Henrique in the Benfica goal no chance.

In most cases the forehead is used to head the ball. After all, it is the flattest part of the head and when the connection with the ball is good it generates power and provides a better chance of accuracy. But power is not the main issue with the glancing header, although accuracy is obviously a priority. The margin for error with this type of header is much greater. A run to the near post and a feeble attempt at a glancing header is an all too common sight. Either the player fails to make enough contact between the side of the head and the inside of the ball, or he 'gets too much' on the ball and meets it full on, sending the ball back in the direction from which it came.

The key to this skill is making the right contact with the right part of the head on the right section of the ball. When you get all three things correct you have a better than even chance of getting your header on target. To score the contact needs to be true in order to get enough pace on the ball to beat a keeper – as our pictures show.

1
You can see the player is going to have to head the ball at an angle of 120 degrees to the cross in order to stand a chance of beating the keeper.

2–3
He does this by glancing the ball with the side of the head and helping the ball goalwards with a twist of the neck.

left
Dutch master Ruud Gullit shows his aerial strength to beat his marker and glance a header goalward.

Tips
i. Time your run, so that you arrive as the ball is at a comfortable height to head.
ii. Keep your eye on the ball rather than the goal.
iii. Try to run across the ball so that you can easily meet it with the side of the head.
iv. Twist your neck as you make contact to steer the ball goalwards.

power shooting

Most goals are scored from inside the penalty area, but a tight defence can make it hard for even the best striker to get in the box. If the 18-yard box is well guarded, the best chance for scoring is a powerful shot from distance. All too often, long range shooting is a case of hit and hope which results in nothing more than embarrassment and lost possession. However with a little composure and a lot of practice, you too can start scoring with 25-yard screamers.

In recent years many players have scored spectacular goals with strikes from distance, but nobody has matched the consistently accurate and powerful strikes of Dutchman Ronald Koeman. The former Barcelona and Holland sweeper developed a faultless technique which brought him goals from both free-kicks and open play. Another player who developed a reputation as dangerous from distance was former Germany skipper Lothar Matthäus. The powerful midfielder inspired West Germany to their World Cup win in 1990, scoring four goals with an immaculate display of powerful shooting.

STRIKING THE BALL

Timing, rather than muscle, is the key to powerful shooting. To strike the ball well, you will need to position your body so that you can easily connect with the 'sweet spot' on the top of the striking foot. The non-kicking foot should be planted firmly alongside the ball to give you a solid base to generate the necessary power in your kicking foot. Strike through the ball in a continuous motion and, to keep the shot down, position your head directly over the ball. If you swipe at the ball and lean back with your head in the air – as many players do – the ball will end up ballooning over the bar rather than nestling in the net.

88 volleying   **90** chip   **92** overhead kick   **94** scissors kick   **96** diving header

Top tip

Don't be afraid to try your luck from long range as you may catch the goalkeeper napping. Once you've decided to shoot, strike the ball with conviction and confidence.

1
The non-kicking foot is planted alongside the ball, the head is over the ball and the outstretched arm provides extra balance.

2
Strike through the ball with conviction, still keeping your head down. Don't just hit and hope; go for accuracy as well as power.

3
The sight of a prostrate goalkeeper and a bulging net is a great feeling for any player.

left
Juventus midfielder Zinedine Zidane lets fly with a left-foot screamer from the edge of the penalty area. Zidane's powerful displays for Juve and France have earned him the nickname 'The Bear' and a reputation as one of the most talented players in the game.

88 volleying   **90** chip   **92** overhead kick   **94** scissors kick   **96** diving header

sending the keeper down

Only the keeper to beat and he must score… but only if he keeps his cool. All too often strikers freeze in one-against-one situations and miss their chance. The art of good finishing is to stay in control and to wait for a good sight of goal before shooting.

Scots master Kenny Dalglish established a reputation as one of the calmest strikers in history during his long career with Celtic, Liverpool and Scotland. Dalglish was never hurried or flustered by an on-rushing keeper and always found the time to measure his finish. In a 12-year spell on Merseyside he scored an impressive 118 goals, but none was more important, or typical, than the goal which won Liverpool the European Cup in Dalglish's first season with the Reds in 1978.

With the score still at 0–0 in the 66th minute, Dalglish received the ball with space to attack the Bruges goal. As the striker moved in on goal the Bruges keeper came off his line, Dalglish stopped his run (as if he was about to shoot) and chipped the ball up and over the stranded keeper from close range to give the Reds the lead and eventually the match.

The chip technique used by Dalglish is an effective, though underused, method of scoring from one-against-one situations. The key is to wait for the keeper to commit himself by feigning to shoot before lifting the ball over the now-grounded goalie.

Tip
Try to deceive the keeper that you are going to strike the ball early by shaping to shoot and stubbing your foot into the ground.

1
Don't be put off as the goalie charges toward you. Delay your shot until he is on his way to ground.

2
Jab at the ball without any follow-through to send it up and over the stranded keeper.

3–4
The goalkeeper had committed himself and is helpless as the ball loops over him and into the unguarded net.

98 scoop   **100** swerve   **102** glancing header   **104** power shooting   **106** sending keeper down   *108* rounding keeper

1

2

rounding the keeper

Faced with an advancing keeper, a striker's options are limited: shoot as he comes off his line, chip him as he goes to ground or try to go around him. All too often players hesitate and are forced into the last option and, because of their hesitancy, they make a mess of it. However, going round the keeper is an excellent option providing you're decisive.

As you approach the keeper you must watch his every move. Try to tempt him to dive and commit himself – one way to do this is to feign to shoot. Alternatively you can give the keeper a good sight of the ball. As he tries to dive toward the ball you must be ready to get the ball out of his reach. You should also try to get your body in his way. By doing this he will either end up stranded or will be forced to foul you and concede a penalty. With the goal at your mercy you must now strike the ball firmly into the middle of the goal. Avoid showing off or delaying

your shot. Showboating can be costly – you may end up being closed down by a defender, or worse still miss the target altogether.

Croatia's Davor Suker provided an example of perfect one-against-one finishing during the quarter finals of Euro 96 against Germany. Faced with the daunting figure of Adreas Kopke, the giant German keeper, the striker rolled his foot over the top of the ball. Kopke dived to the ground thinking that Suker was about to shoot. With the big keeper now committed, Suker was left with a clear sight of goal and the simple task of stroking the ball into an empty net. A simple goal which combined both speed of thought and fast feet.

Top Tip
Don't panic and change your mind as the keeper comes out. The chances are that if you try and shoot he'll be in a position to block.

1
The keeper rushes off his line to close down the striker who is bearing down on goal.

2
The striker rolls his foot over the ball as the keeper dives and brings it out of the goalie's reach.

3
The keeper is left stranded and the striker wastes no time in stroking the ball into the unprotected net.

left
Brazilian striker Romario uses his excellent balance to stay on his feet and score, despite the desperate challenge of Italian keeper Pagliuca.

98 scoop   **100** swerve   **102** glancing header   **104** power shooting   **106** sending keeper down   **108** rounding keeper

A

Ardiles flick 29
Ardiles, Osvaldo 29
Asprilla, Faustino 19

B

Baggio, Dino 35
Baggio, Roberto 36-37, 62
Baia, Vitor 98
Basic technique 10-19
Bayern Munich 42
Beardsley feint 7, 76-77
Beardsley, Peter 7, 44, 77
Beckanbauer, Franz 9, 74
Beckham, David 56, 57, 60, 91
Bergkamp, Dennis 73
Best, George 7, 8, 68, 72, 74, 92
Blanchflower, Danny 7
Boban, Zvonimir 85
Bogarde, Winston 42
Brehme, Andy 96
Bremner, Billy 47
Brolin, Tomas 58

C

Cantona, Eric 7, 13, 62
Carlos, Roberto 56
Carr, Willie 54
Charlton, Bobby 64, 88, 92, 103
Chest control 16
Chipping for goal 90-91, 98
Corners 40
Corners, whipped-in 60-61
Cruyff turn 7, 8, 10, 74, 75, 78
Cruyff, Johan 8, 74, 75

D

Dalglish, Kenny 107
Dasaev, Rinat 88
Davies, Hunter 7
Double drag back 73
Drag back 8, 72
Dummy 68
Dunne, Tony 103

E

Eusebio 103
Escape to Victory 29

F

Finishing 88-109
First touch
    Inside of the foot 15
    Sole of the foot 15
    Top of the foot 15
Five-a-side football 35
Free-kicks
    Bending 56-57
    Flick-up and volley 54-55
    Passed 58-59

G

Garrincha 56
Gascoigne, Paul 7, 57, 74, 78, 79
Giggs, Ryan 60, 100
Ginola, David 42, 85, 92, 93
Gray, Andy 96
Gullit, Ruud 61, 103

H

Hässler, Thomas 56
Head tennis 19
Headers
    Attacking 19
    Defensive 19
    Diving 96-97
    Glancing 102-103
Hendry, Colin 78
Hoddle, Glenn 7, 49
Hughes, Mark 38
Hunt, Ernie 54
Hutchinson, Ian 52

J

Jairzinho 74
Johnny Giles 47
Juggling
    Back of heel 26-27
    Foot catch 24
    Neck catch 26-27
    Thigh 24-25
Juninho 70, 82, 85

K

Keegan, Kevin 40, 94
Kelly, Alan 65
Klinsmann, Jürgen 94, 96
Koeman, Ronald 62, 104
Kohler, Jürgen 40
Kopke, Andreas 108

INDEX

L
Law, Denis 92
Le Tissier, Matt 54
Legg, Andy 52
Lineker, Gary 64

M
Maldini, Paolo 15
Maradona 8, 44
Matthäus, Lothar 10
Matthews, Stanley 68, 69
McAlliog, Jim 54
Moller, Andreas 35
Muhren, Arnold 88
Müller, Gerd 96

N
Nayim 91
Nutmeg 80-81

O
Osgood, Peter 54
Overhead kick 92-93
Overmars, Marc 70

P
Pagliuca, Gianluca 108
Papin, Jean Pierre 7
Passing
    Back heel 47
    Chest pass 38
    Chipped pass 48
    Disguised pass 44
    Inside of the foot 13, 42
    Outside of the foot 13
    Scissors pass 36
    Side foot 12, 42
    Swerve pass 42, 48
    Top of the foot 13
    Wall pass 34
Pele 8, 74
Penalties 62-65
Penalties, chipped 64-65
Peruzzi, Angelo 56
Pincer flick 31
Platini, Michel 8
Poborsky, Karel 98, 99
Power shooting 104-105

R
Radford, John 52
Reid, Peter 96
Rivelino 56
Rolling foot over ball 84-85
Romario 38, 109
Round the corner flick 82-83
Rounding the keeper 108-109
Rumminegge, Karl-Heinz 96

S
Sanchez, Hugo 92
Scissors kick 94-95, 96
Scoop 98
Seaman, David 91
Sending keeper down 106-107
Set-plays 50-64
Shearer, Alan 57
Sheringham, Teddy 40
Southall, Neville 94
Step-over 8, 70
Stop-start move 78
Suker, Davor 108
Sullivan, Neil 91
Swansea City 52
Swerve shot 100

T
Taffarel 64
The Glory Game 7
Thigh control 16
Throw-in, long 52-53
Toe punt 13
Toshack, John 40
Tournoi de France 56
Van Basten, Marco 88

V
Vialli, Gianluca 88
Volleying 88-89

W
Waddle, Chris 6-7

Y
Yorke, Dwight 64, 65

Z
Zidane, Zinedine 100, 104
Ziege, Christian 42
Zola, Gianfranco 42, 44, 56, 60, 100

All photo's: **Reed International Books/Alex Henderson** except for the following:

Action Images

15 bottom, 64 bottom, 85 bottom, 102 top right.

Allsport

Clive Brunskill 78, David Cannon 44 bottom left, Phil Cole 42 top left, Laurence Griffiths 77 top left, M. Prior 54 left, Ben Radford 91 bottom right, 99 bottom, 109 bottom left, Pascal Rondeau 42 bottom left, Mark Thompson 93 top right, Claudio Villa 37 top, Anton Want 105

Allsport Historical Collection

Front Endpaper, 68 bottom left, 74-75 bottom, 95 top

Colorsport

6, 49 bottom, 56 bottom left /Olympia /Aldo Martinuzzi 61 bottom

PHOTOGRAPHIC ACKNOWLEDGEMENTS